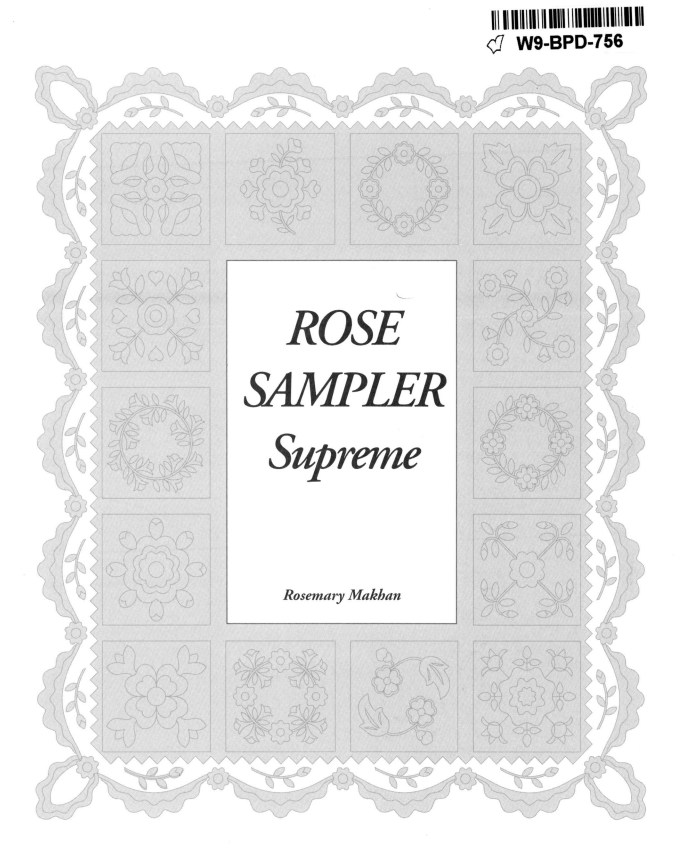

ROSE SAMPLER
Supreme

Rosemary Makhan

Martingale
& COMPANY

That Patchwork Place is an imprint of
Martingale & Company.

Rose Sampler Supreme
© 1999 by Rosemary Makhan

Martingale & Company
20205 144th Avenue NE
Woodinville, WA 98072-8478 USA
www.martingale-pub.com

Printed in the United States of America
06 05 04   11 10 9 8 7 6

CREDITS

President .... Nancy J. Martin
CEO/Publisher .... Daniel J. Martin
Associate Publisher .... Jane Hamada
Editorial Director .... Mary V. Green
Design & Production Manager .... Cheryl Stevenson
Technical Editor .... Ursula Reikes
Copy Editor .... Liz McGehee
Illustrator .... Laurel Strand
Photographer .... Brent Kane
Designer .... Cheryl Stevenson

MISSION STATEMENT

We are dedicated to providing quality products and service by working together to inspire creativity and to enrich the lives we touch.

Dedication

To the memory of my dear friend and quilting buddy, Sylvia McMillan. Sylvia took one of my early Rose Sampler quilting classes, and we shared many happy days fabric hunting and sewing together at each other's homes. I'll really miss our times together.

Acknowledgments

My sincere appreciation to:

Peggy Gelbrich and Barbara Green for sharing their award-winning quilts in this book.

Carol Cunningham of The Quilt Batt for expertly machine quilting the Rose Sampler Twelve-Block Variation.

My husband, Chris, for his patience and tolerance of yet another project. He's getting pretty good at getting meals ready, too.

For all those who took my Rose Sampler classes—your support and encouragement meant a great deal.

For all those appliqué lovers who kept requesting that the pattern be reprinted—it's because of you that this book became a reality.

That Patchwork Place/Martingale & Company for deciding to reprint the pattern pack as a book.

Library of Congress Cataloging-in-Publication Data

Makhan, Rosemary
    Rose sampler supreme / Rosemary Makhan.
       p. cm.
    ISBN 1-56477-316-7
    1. Appliqué—Patterns. 2. Quilts. 3. Roses in art. I. Title

TT779.M25 1999
746.46'041—dc21   99-051339

Table of Contents

Introduction

I am a rose of Sharon,
a lily of the valleys.
As a lily among brambles,
so is my love among maidens.
As an apple tree among the trees of the wood,
so is my beloved among young men.
Song of Solomon 2:1–3
(Revised Standard Version)

Bible scholars tell us that the Song of Solomon is a love song expounding the joys of wedded life. In Chapter 2, the bride tells us of her delight in the love of King Solomon.

Throughout the years, the Rose of Sharon quilt patterns have been the most popular for bridal quilts due to their beauty and to their symbolism of romantic love.

There are many rose-pattern variations, but all are characterized by layered rose flowers and leaves, and many have rosebuds or blossoms. Often, these rose patterns have other names as well, but probably all were originally based on the Rose of Sharon, which is now considered an appliqué quilt pattern. Similar rose patterns also abound on textiles, wallpaper, rugs, crewelwork, and china.

In the early days of our country, when needlework skills were essential, it was expected that every young girl would have several quilts made for her dowry. When she became engaged (and not before—for it was feared bad luck), she would start her bridal quilt. The design selected was most often a Rose of Sharon pattern, and the quilt was made with great care and patience. Because of their great beauty in design and workmanship, bridal quilts were used only on very special occasions and were passed down as cherished family heirlooms. As a result, many of these beautiful quilts survive in family and museum collections.

The Rose Sampler Supreme quilt is a modern version of these heirloom-quality quilts. It features twenty 14" appliquéd blocks, each a Rose of Sharon variation, plus a graceful swag border accented with inner and outer appliquéd dogtooth edgings. Enjoy making your special version of this beautiful quilt. Feel free to interpret it in color combinations other than the soft pink and green tones in the quilt pictured on the cover.

Quiltmaking Basics

Supplies

◆**SEWING MACHINE:** To machine piece, you'll need a sewing machine that has a good straight stitch. You'll also need a walking foot or darning foot if you are going to machine quilt.

◆**ROTARY-CUTTING TOOLS:** You will need a rotary cutter, cutting mat, and clear acrylic rulers in a variety of sizes, including 6" x 24" and 12" x 12".

◆**THREAD:** Use a good-quality, all-purpose cotton or cotton-covered polyester thread. Make sure that the thread you use is strong, but save your quilting thread for the quilting process. It is thicker than all-purpose thread and will show if you use it for appliqué.

Thread used for appliqué should match the color of the appliqué pieces rather than the color of the background fabric. Designs with many different-colored pieces require many shades of thread. If you can't match the color exactly, choose thread that is a little darker than the fabric. If the appliqué fabric contains many colors, choose a neutral-colored thread that blends with the predominant color.

White or light-colored thread should always be used for basting. Dye from dark thread can leave small dots of color on light fabrics.

◆**NEEDLES:** For machine piecing, a size 10/70 or 12/80 works well for most cottons.

For hand appliqué, size 10 (fine) to size 12 (very fine) needles work well.

◆**PINS:** Long, fine "quilters' pins" with glass or plastic heads are easy to handle. Small ½"- to ¾"-long sequin pins work well for appliqué.

◆**SCISSORS:** Use your best scissors to cut fabric only. Use an older pair of scissors to cut paper, cardboard, and template plastic. Small, 4" scissors with sharp points are handy for clipping thread.

◆**TEMPLATE PLASTIC:** Use clear or frosted plastic (available at quilt shops) to make durable, accurate templates.

◆**SEAM RIPPER:** Use this tool to remove stitches from incorrectly sewn seams.

◆**MARKING TOOLS:** Use a sharp No. 2 pencil or fine-lead mechanical pencil on lighter-colored fabrics, and a silver or white marking pencil on darker fabrics. Chalk pencils or chalk-wheel markers also make clear marks on fabric. Be sure to test your marking tool to make sure you can remove the marks easily.

Fabrics

Most quilters like to use all-cotton fabrics. They hold their shape and are easy to handle. Cottons blended with polyester or other fibers may tend to slip, slide, or unravel as you sew them together. Sometimes, however, a favorite fabric is worth a little extra care as you sew it into your quilt. Your enjoyment as you stitch the pretty colors into your design will outweigh the extra attention that may be necessary to control the fabric.

When choosing fabric for appliqué, you need fabric for two purposes: the background fabric and the appliqué pieces. Background fabrics are usually solid, light colors or small prints and stripes that complement the appliqué design. White-on-white printed fabrics make lovely appliqué backgrounds. Using a bold print, plaid, or stripe as the background fabric may detract from the appliquéd design.

Fabrics used for the appliqué pieces should be appropriate for the design. Consider the proper color and print size for the pattern you are stitching. Solid fabrics are always "safe" to use, but printed fabrics can make your design more exciting. Little floral prints and geometric calicoes work well. Fabrics printed in shades of one color can be very effective for representing texture in flowers, leaves, and other natural shapes. Large multicolored fabrics may be too elaborate for small appliqué pieces. The design in a large-print fabric becomes lost in a small appliqué piece, although sometimes you can cut a perfect design from a specific area of a large print. Avoid stripes and plaids unless they work well with your design.

Prewash all fabrics to prevent shrinking and bleeding in the quilt. Wash dark and light colors separately with laundry detergent so that the dark colors do not run onto the light colors. Sometimes, it is necessary to rinse dark fabrics a few times, until the color stops bleeding and the rinse water is clear. Iron the fabrics until they are smooth, so the pieces will be accurate when they are cut. Using a spray starch or sizing helps give fabrics extra body and makes them easier to handle.

Rotary Cutting

All measurements include standard ¼"-wide seam allowances. For those unfamiliar with rotary cutting, a brief introduction is provided. For more detailed information, see Donna Thomas's *Shortcuts: A Concise Guide to Rotary Cutting* (That Patchwork Place).

1. Fold the fabric and match selvages, aligning the crosswise and lengthwise grains as much as possible. Place the folded edge closest to you on the cutting mat. Align a square ruler along the folded edge of the fabric. Place a long, straight ruler to the left of the square ruler, just covering the uneven raw edges on the left side of the fabric.

   Remove the square ruler and cut along the right edge of the long ruler, rolling the rotary cutter away from you. Discard this strip. (Reverse this procedure if you are left-handed.)

   Selvages

2. To cut strips, align the required measurement on the ruler with the newly cut edge of the fabric. For example, to cut a 3"-wide strip, place the 3" ruler mark on the edge of the fabric.

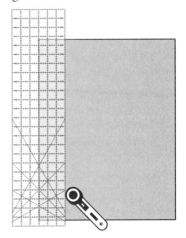

3. To cut squares, cut strips in the required widths. Trim away the selvage ends of the strip. Align the required measurement on the ruler with the left edge of the strip and cut a square. Continue cutting squares until you have the number needed.

Pressing

The traditional rule in quiltmaking is to press seams to one side, toward the darker color wherever possible. Before pressing the seam to one side, press the seam flat from the wrong side as it comes from the sewing machine; this relaxes the thread and smooths out any puckers. Then turn the piece over and press the seam in the desired direction from the right side. Press carefully to avoid distorting the shapes.

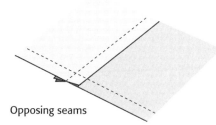

Opposing seams

When joining two seamed units, plan ahead and press the seam allowances in opposite directions as shown. This reduces bulk and makes it easier to match seam lines. Where two seams meet, the seam allowances will butt against each other, making it easier to join units with perfectly matched seam intersections.

Appliqué

Instructions are provided for three different appliqué methods: traditional, needle-turn, and freezer-paper appliqué. Choose one of these or use your favorite method. It may be helpful to read through all the methods before beginning.

Making Templates

Templates made from clear plastic are more durable and accurate than those made from cardboard. Since you can see through the plastic, it is easy to trace the templates accurately.

Place template plastic over each pattern piece and trace with a fine-line permanent marker. Do not add seam allowances. Cut out the templates on the drawn lines. You need only one template for each different design. Mark the pattern name and grain-line arrow (if applicable) on the template. Templates are not necessary for the freezer-paper method on page 10.

Marking and Cutting Fabric

Place the templates right side up on the right side of the appliqué fabric. Draw around the shapes. Leave at least ½" between shapes. Cut out each piece, adding a scant ¼"-wide seam allowance beyond the drawn line. This seam allowance will be turned under to create the finished edge of the appliqué. On very small pieces, you may wish to add only ⅛" for easier handling.

The background fabric is usually a rectangle or square. Cut fabric the size and shape required for each project. If yardage allows, it is better to cut the background slightly larger than needed in each direction to start, then trim it to the correct size after the appliqué has been sewn in place on the background fabric.

When positioning the prepared appliqués on the background block, fold the block into quarters and then diagonally. Crease lightly with your fingers or gently with an iron so that these lines can be used as a guide when basting the shapes in place. You may place the block pattern underneath the background blocks as a positioning guide if you wish.

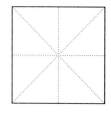

Use crease lines as a guide
for appliqué placement.

Another method is to place the background fabric right side up over the pattern so that the design is centered. Lightly trace the design with a pencil. If your background fabric is dark, use a light box, or try taping the pattern to a window or storm door on a sunny day.

Traditional Appliqué Method

Before sewing appliqués to the background, turn under the seam allowance, rolling the drawn line to the back. Baste around each piece. Try looking at the right side of the piece while you turn the edge under, basting right along the fold to catch the seam allowance.

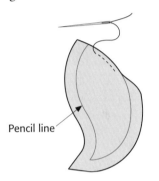

Pencil line

Do not turn under edges that will be covered by other appliqué pieces. These edges should lie flat.

Do not turn under this edge.

Pin or baste the appliqué pieces to the background fabric. If you have trouble with threads tangling around pins as you sew, try placing the pins on the underside of your work.

TRADITIONAL APPLIQUÉ STITCH

The traditional appliqué stitch or blind stitch is appropriate for sewing all appliqué shapes, including sharp points and curves.

1. Tie a knot in a single strand of thread that is approximately 18" long.

2. Hide the knot by slipping the needle into the seam allowance from the wrong side of the appliqué piece, bringing it out on the fold line.

3. Work from right to left if you are right-handed, or left to right if you are left-handed. Start the first stitch by moving the needle straight off the appliqué, inserting the needle into the background fabric. Let the needle travel under the background fabric, parallel to the edge of the appliqué; bring it up about ⅛" away, along the pattern line.

4. As you bring the needle up, pierce the edge of the appliqué piece, catching only one or two threads of the folded edge.

5. Move the needle straight off the appliqué into the background fabric. Let your needle travel under the background, bringing it up about ⅛" away, again catching the edge of the appliqué.

6. Give the thread a slight tug and continue stitching.

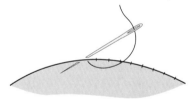

Appliqué Stitch

7. To end your stitching, pull the needle through to the wrong side. Behind the appliqué piece, take 2 small stitches, making knots by taking your needle through the loops. Check the right side to see if the thread "shadows" through the background. If it does, take 1 more small stitch on the back side to direct the tail of the thread under the appliqué fabric.

STITCHING OUTSIDE POINTS

As you stitch toward an outside point, start taking smaller stitches within ½" of the point. Trim the seam allowance or push the excess fabric under the point with the tip of your needle. Smaller stitches near the point will keep any frayed edges from escaping.

Place the last stitch on the first side very close to the point. Place the next stitch on the second side of the point. A stitch on each side, close to the point, will accent the outside point.

Sometimes these areas can be reinforced with a liquid seam sealant to retard fraying after stitching them in place. If you wish to try this, test the sealant first on a scrap of the same fabric to make sure it dries clear without changing the color of the fabric.

STITCHING ALONG A CURVE

Push the fabric under with the tip of your needle, smoothing it out along the folded edge before sewing.

STITCHING INSIDE POINTS

Make your stitches smaller as you sew within ½" of the point. Stitch past the point, then return to the point to add one extra stitch to emphasize it. Come up through the appliqué, catching a little more fabric in the inside point (four or five threads instead of one or two). Make a straight stitch outward, going under the point to pull it in a little and emphasize its shape.

If your inside point frays, use a few close stitches to tack the fabric down securely. If your thread matches your appliqué fabric, these stitches will blend in with the edge of the shape.

Alternate Appliqué Methods

NEEDLE-TURN APPLIQUÉ

This method moves directly from cutting to the appliqué stitch. You do not turn under and baste the seam allowances.

1. Place the plastic template on the right side of the appliqué fabric. Draw around the shape.
2. Cut out the fabric piece, adding a scant ¼"-wide seam allowance all around.
3. Position the appliqué piece on the background fabric; pin or baste in place.
4. Starting on a straight edge, use the tip of the needle to gently turn under the seam allowance, about ½" at a time. Hold the turned seam allowance firmly between the thumb and first finger of your left hand (reverse if left-handed) as you stitch the appliqué to the background. Use a longer needle—a Sharp or milliner's needle—to help you control the seam allowance and turn it under neatly.

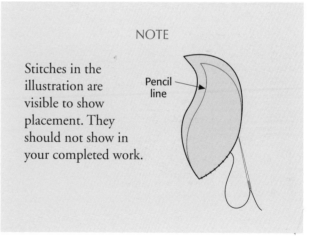

NOTE

Stitches in the illustration are visible to show placement. They should not show in your completed work.

Pencil line

FREEZER-PAPER APPLIQUÉ

Use freezer paper (plastic-coated on one side) to help make perfectly shaped appliqués. You can trace around a template or simply trace the design onto freezer paper. The seam allowances are then turned over the freezer-paper edges and basted or glued to the back side before appliquéing the shape to the background. (See "Freezer Paper Appliqué Tips" on page 11.)

1. Place freezer paper, plastic side down, on top of the pattern and trace the design with a sharp pencil.

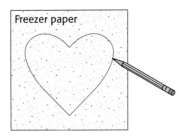

2. Cut out the freezer-paper design on the pencil line. Do not add seam allowances.

3. With the plastic-coated side against the wrong side of the fabric, iron the freezer paper in place, using a hot, dry iron.

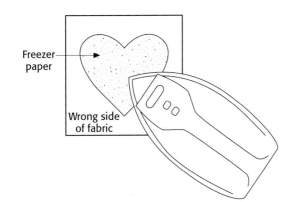

4. Cut out the shape, adding ¼"-wide seam allowances around the outside edge of the freezer paper.

5. Turn and baste the seam allowance over the freezer-paper edges by hand, or use a gluestick. (Clip inside points and fold outside points.)

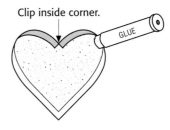

Clip inside corner.

6. Pin or baste the design to the background fabric. Appliqué the design.

7. Remove any basting stitches. Cut a small slit in the background fabric behind the appliqué. If you used a gluestick, soak the piece in warm water for a few minutes to release the freezer paper. Remove the freezer paper with tweezers.

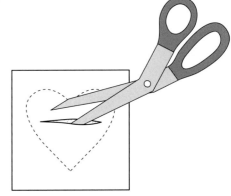

Bias Bars

Many appliqué patterns include stems or linear elements, which require narrow strips of fabric. The following technique provides a virtually foolproof method to create beautiful, perfect stems and strips.

1. To determine the cut width of the bias fabric to be appliquéd, double the width of the finished strip and add ⅝". (For example, if you want a ¼" finished strip, double ¼" (½") and add ⅝" to equal 1⅛".) Cut bias strips to your desired width and join end to end, if necessary, for a longer strip.

Freezer-Paper Appliqué Tips

◆ Asymmetrical designs must be traced onto the freezer paper from the reverse or back side of the pattern. This is necessary only occasionally in the blocks for this quilt. A good example is the asymmetrical leaf shape in Pattern #19, Wild Rose. Place the pattern with the right side against a light table or tape it to a window so the design shadows through for easy tracing.

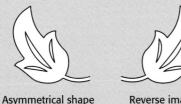

Asymmetrical shape   Reverse image

◆ Cut the leaves with reverse appliqué in Patterns #4 (Lancaster Rose) and #19 (Wild Rose) from the freezer paper. Then cut out the interior shapes from the freezer paper.

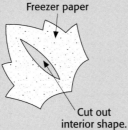

Freezer paper

Cut out
interior shape.

Press the freezer paper to the wrong side of the fabric. Cut out, adding seam allowances around the outside edges, and prepare the appliqué as shown in "Freezer-Paper Appliqué," opposite. In the reverse appliqué area, slash the fabric and turn the raw edges in, over the edge of the cutout in the freezer paper, trimming and clipping the fabric as needed for a smoothly turned edge.

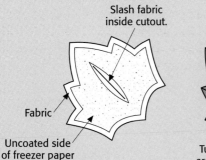

Slash fabric
inside cutout.

Fabric

Uncoated side
of freezer paper

Turn fabric to inside
around cutout edges.

When the appliqué is stitched to the block, the background fabric will show through the hole. Or, a different fabric can be placed behind the hole if desired.

Background
shows through.

◆ Only clip the seam allowances where necessary for smoothly turned edges. Too many clips weaken the seam and make it more difficult to achieve smooth edges on your appliqué shapes. Clip sharp indents almost to the freezer paper.

Clip to freezer paper.

◆ To create a sharp point on appliqués, such as on the small leaves in Pattern #1 (Indiana Rose), first fold the seam allowance directly across the tip of the leaf. Then fold the seam allowances in from both sides to miter the corner. If any of the seam allowances extend beyond the leaf shape at the tip, trim them at an angle.

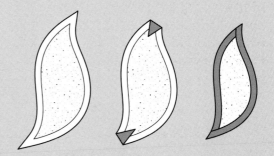

2. Fold the bias strip lengthwise, wrong sides together, and stitch slightly more than the desired width from the fold. (For example, for a ¼" finished strip, stitch ¼" plus one or two threads from the fold.) Trim the seam allowances if necessary. (For the ¼" bias strip, I trimmed the seam allowances to ⅛" after stitching the seam.)

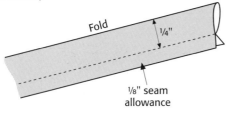

3. Slip the bias bar into the tube created by stitching. The fabric tube should fit snugly.

4. Twist the fabric tube to center the seam on the bias bar. The seam allowances should not overlap the edge of the bias bar.

5. Using steam, press in this position—while the fabric tube is on the bias bar. The seam side is now the "wrong" side of the bias strip (the side that will lie next to the background fabric). Be careful! Metal bias bars become very hot from the iron!

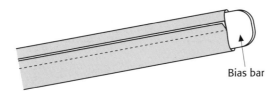

6. Remove the bias bar from the strip and press the strip on the other (right) side. Your bias strip is ready to appliqué.

NOTE
If your finished strip will be appliquéd as a curved strip, carefully curve the strip as you are ironing it to provide a smoother curve to the finished bias strip. When appliquéing, stitch the inner curve of the strip first, then the outer curve.

Embroidery

Embroidery is often used to add details to appliqué or patchwork. Many quilters embroider the information on their quilt labels.

◆NEEDLES: Crewel needles from size 8 to 10 are wonderful for embroidery. They have large eyes to make it easier to thread several strands of embroidery floss. The smaller size will help you create more delicate stitches; if your needle is too thick, it may distort the stitches as it moves through the fabric.

◆THREAD: Embroidery floss comes in a variety of colors. The six strands of floss can be separated for more delicate designs.

◆HOOP: An embroidery hoop will keep your fabric stretched out and smooth as you sew. The fabric should be tight over your hoop, so the fabric will not be distorted by the stitches. Remove the hoop when you are not stitching, to avoid unwanted marks on your fabric.

Stem Stitch

The stem stitch is used as an outline stitch or to stitch straight lines, such as flower stems.

To begin stitching, tie a knot in the end of the two strands of embroidery floss. Cut the tail short so that the floss will not shadow through to the front of the quilt.

1. Bring the needle up through the fabric at point A. Insert the needle at B, approximately ¼" away, and come up again at C, halfway between A and B. Pull the thread through, holding the thread below the needle.

2. To continue the stitch, insert the needle at D, and come up again at B, the same place where the needle went into the fabric for the last stitch. Pull the thread through, always holding the thread below the needle.

3. Continue by repeating step 2. Each stitch will touch the previous stitch.

Stem Stitch

Rose Sampler Supreme

Rose Sampler Supreme

FINISHED QUILT SIZE: 84" X 100"

MATERIALS: 42"-WIDE FABRIC

NOTE: If you prefer to add more variety, use small amounts of other coordinating fabrics in addition to those listed.

Cream 7¼ yds. plain or printed muslin or broadcloth for blocks and borders

pink 3¾ yds. small-scale dusty rose print (pindot or other small unobtrusive print) for flowers, inner dog tooth edging, sashing, and swags

Lt/dk pink ½ yd. each of 2 medium-scale coordinating prints in dusty rose for flowers and buds

pink print 1½ yds. larger-scale dusty rose print for border swags and block flowers

dk gr 3 yds. green print for outer dogtooth edging, binding, leaves, and stems

dk greens med Lt 1 yd. each of 3 assorted green prints for leaves and stems

6 yds. for backing

88" x 104" low-loft batting

NOTE: There should be a total of 4 dusty rose prints (be sure to vary the value and the scale of the prints) and 4 green prints.

CUTTING

◆ All measurements are cut sizes and include ¼"-wide seam allowances.

◆ Cut sizes for border strips and long sashing strips are 2" longer than the required length; the excess will be trimmed later.

◆ Do not include selvages in any of the pieces.

◆ Label the pieces after you cut them to avoid getting them mixed up or cutting into them for another project.

◆ Cut the borders, sashing strips, and dogtooth edgings first and set them aside. From the remaining fabrics, cut the appliqué pieces for each block, and the swag, flowers, and leaves for the border.

From the fabric for blocks and borders, cut:

20 squares, each 15" x 15" for blocks. The blocks will be trimmed to 14½" x 14½" after appliqué is complete.

From the remaining fabric for blocks and borders, cut:

2 strips, each 10½" x 86" for outer top and bottom borders.

2 strips, each 10½" x 102", for outer side borders.

NOTE: If your fabric measures more than 42" wide after preshrinking, divide the actual width by 4 and use that measurement for the cut width of the border strips. For example, if your fabric measures 44", cut the border strips each 11" wide instead of 10½" wide.

From the small-scale dusty rose print, cut on the length-wise grain:

6 strips, each 2½" x 64½", for horizontal sashing and inner top and bottom dogtooth edgings

2 strips, each 2½" x 80½", for inner side dogtooth edgings

From the remaining small-scale dusty rose print, cut:

15 pieces, each 2½" x 14½", for vertical sashing strips

From the 3 yds. of green print, cut:

2 strips, each 2½" x 90½", for outer top and bottom dogtooth edgings (includes 6" extra for mitering corners)

2 strips, each 2½" x 106½", for outer side dogtooth edgings (includes 6" extra for mitering corners)

Enough 2½"-wide straight-grain strips to make a 376"-long binding strip when joined

DIRECTIONS

Patterns for the blocks are on pages 25–32 and 49–72.

Appliqué the Blocks

1. Cut and prepare the appliqués, using the appliqué method you prefer. I used the freezer-paper method to prepare the appliqués for the quilt shown in the photograph and I highly recommend it. If you plan to use this method, read the basic directions first and then study the tips in the box on page 11 before cutting and preparing the appliqués for each block.

   NOTE: It's a good idea to cut and prepare the swags, flowers, and buds for the borders before making too many blocks, just to be sure you are cutting your fabric to best advantage.

2. Stitch appliqués in place, following the instructions for "Traditional Appliqué Stitch" on page 8. Use thread that closely matches the color of the appliqué and make your stitches as invisible as possible. If you are using the freezer-paper method, try to stitch only through to the layer directly below the appliqué shape, not all the other layers beneath it. This makes removal of the paper much easier.

3. When all stitching is complete (and the freezer paper has been removed), trim away the excess fabric behind each appliqué shape, leaving a ¼" allowance all around. This eliminates extra bulk and makes quilting easier.

Assemble the Quilt Top

PLEASE NOTE: ALL SEAM ALLOWANCES ARE ¼" WIDE.

1. Sew the blocks together in 5 horizontal rows, joining them with the short vertical sashing strips between. Refer to the quilt photo for block placement, but feel free to rearrange the blocks to your liking. Press all seam allowances toward the sashing strips.

2. Assemble the rows into the quilt top, joining the rows of blocks with horizontal sashing strips. To prevent stretching, mark the sashing strips with the block width and sashing width, alternating them as shown. Note that the block dimensions at each side are ¼" larger because no seam allowance has been taken yet.

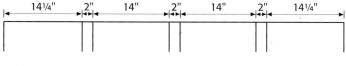

3. Pin the sashing strips to the block rows, carefully matching the marks to the appropriate seams. Stitch, then trim any excess sashing strip.

Add the Dogtooth Edgings

1. Prepare and attach the strips for the dusty rose inner dogtooth edgings. Turn under and press ¼" along one long edge of each dusty rose strip. On the wrong side, draw a line 1" from the remaining long raw edge on each strip.

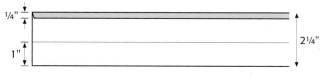

2. Beginning 1" in from one short end of each strip, mark and cut slits 2" apart. Cut from the pressed edge to, but not past, the 1" marking. This will create a "flap" for each dogtooth. On each sashing strip, you should have a total of 7 flaps for each block and 1 for each sashing strip.

3. Fold cut flaps in from each side and press to form a triangle for each dogtooth. The flaps will overlap. Make sure the tip of each triangle is centered in the 2" flap and be very careful to press so that each triangle shape comes sharply down to a point on both sides at the base line (1" marking). Use gluestick sparingly to glue the overlapping flaps in place.

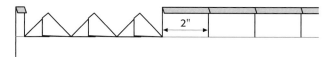

4. Fold each of the prepared dogtooth strips and each of the 4 background border strips in half crosswise and mark the center of each strip. Pin each of the prepared dogtooth strips to a corresponding border strip, matching centers and allowing the long raw edge of the dogtooth strip to extend ½" beyond the raw edge of the border strip. You may use gluestick to hold it in place.

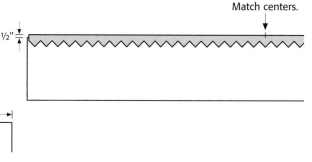

5. Hand appliqué the dogtooth strips in place, being careful to take several stitches very close together at the base line of each dogtooth.

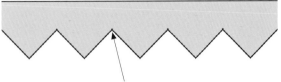

Take several tiny stitches at the inner points.

6. Prepare and sew the outer green dogtooth edgings in a similar manner. At both ends of each outer dogtooth strip, there will be 4 extra dogtooths and 1 partial dogtooth, plus additional length to allow for mitering at the corners.

NOTE: To make sure the outer dogtooth edgings will fit your border exactly, wait to mark and cut the last five corner dogtooth divisions at each end of the border strips until you actually place each strip on the outer border. Work from the center out to mark and cut the same number of flaps on the outer strips as you did on the inner dogtooth strips.

Attach the Borders

1. Pin the borders to the quilt top. As you pin, match the dogtooth divisions to the block and sashing divisions.

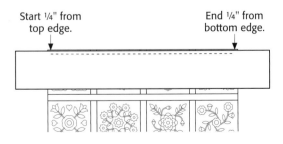

Stitch, beginning and ending each border seam ¼" from the raw edge of the quilt. Press the seams toward the borders.

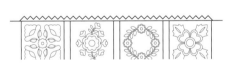

Start ¼" from top edge.   End ¼" from bottom edge.

2. Miter the corners. See "Mitered-Corner Borders" on page 21.
3. Trim away the border fabric behind the dogtooth strips, leaving a ¼"-wide allowance if desired. To eliminate excess bulk, trim the areas that overlap behind the triangles, leaving a ¼"-wide allowance.

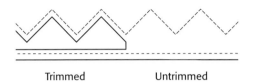

Trimmed   Untrimmed

Add Border Appliqués

1. Cut and prepare the swag, flower, and rosebud appliqué shapes from the patterns provided.
2. Referring to the quilt photo for positioning, use gluestick to hold the prepared shapes in place on the border strips.
3. Appliqué these shapes in place.

Mark the Quilting Patterns

Refer to "Marking the Quilting Lines" on page 22. Full-size quilting patterns for the sashing and border are provided.

1. Mark the heart and feather pattern on the sashing pieces, centering the four-heart cluster at the sashing intersections. The feathers should extend halfway into each adjoining sashing, ending at the midpoint of a block.

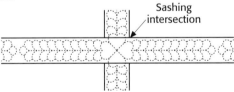

Sashing intersection

2. Mark diagonal quilting lines ¾" apart in the background of each block as shown, but do not mark the lines through the appliqué shapes. Solid lines represent crease lines in the block to help in positioning the quilting lines.

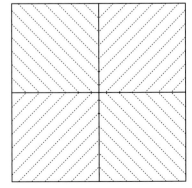

3. Mark the border feather swags, centering them along the outer edge of the appliquéd swags, with the hearts opposite the appliquéd flowers.

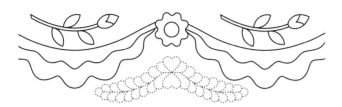

4. Mark crosshatch lines on the remaining border background, using the dogtooth points as a guide for placement as shown. Do not mark through the appliqué shapes (which are not shown in the illustration).

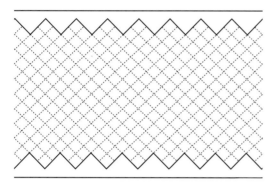

5. Mark parallel lines inside the corner swag pieces as shown.

Finish the Quilt

1. Prepare the quilt backing and batting, following the directions on page 22.
2. Layer the marked quilt top with batting and backing. Baste.
3. Quilt on the marked lines.

4. Outline-quilt ⅛" away from each appliqué shape.

5. Bind the quilt edges with the green, straight-cut binding, mitering the corners. Refer to "Binding" on page 24.
6. Make a label for the back of your quilt, using the method of your choice. Include your name, where the quilt was made, the date, and any other pertinent information. If you wish, use the pattern below to decorate the corners of your label. Use it in all four corners, in just one corner, or in two opposite corners. Use a stem stitch to embroider it, or use a fine-tip, permanent marker to trace it directly onto the label. Heat-set the tracing with an iron before attaching the label to the back of the quilt.

Congratulations on completing a beautiful heirloom quilt that your family will treasure for years to come!

Rose Sampler Twelve-Block Variation

FINISHED QUILT SIZE: 72" x 88"

This simplified version of the Rose Sampler Supreme quilt is quicker and easier, making it suitable for gift giving or for quilters with less experience. Choose twelve of your favorite blocks. The same fabrics are used in each block so the fabric decisions are easy and straightforward. The dogtooth edging is eliminated, and the border is simplified by cutting the swag from just one fabric and eliminating the rosebuds.

MATERIALS: 42"-WIDE FABRIC

5½ yds. plain or printed cream broadcloth for blocks and borders

1¼ yds. burgundy print for sashing*

¼ yd. light burgundy tone-on-tone print for cornerstones

2½ yds. large-scale burgundy print for block flowers and border swags

¼ yd. small-scale burgundy print for flowers and flower centers

1½ yds. large-scale green tone-on-tone print for leaves and stems

½ yd. light burgundy tone-on-tone print for flowers (can be same print as cornerstones)

5½ yds. for backing

¾ yd. burgundy print for binding

76" x 92" low-loft batting

If you prefer to use a striped fabric as shown (with the stripe repeated 4 times across the fabric width), you will need at least 4 yards. When using a stripe, center the same design on each sashing piece for best results.

CUTTING

All measurements are cut sizes and include ¼"-wide seam allowances.

From the broadcloth, cut on the lengthwise grain first:
2 border strips, each 10½" x 74", for top and bottom borders
2 border strips, each 10½" x 90", for side borders.

From the remaining broadcloth, cut:
12 squares, each 14½" x 14½" for blocks. These will be trimmed to 14" x 14" after appliqué is complete.

From the burgundy sashing print, cut:
11 strips, each 3¼" wide, across the fabric width. Crosscut into 31 pieces, each 14" long.
Or, from striped sashing fabric, cut 31 pieces, each 3¼" x 14", carefully cutting along the printed lines on the fabric.

From the burgundy tone-on-tone print, cut:
2 strips, each 3¼" wide, across the fabric width. Crosscut into 20 cornerstones, each 3¼" x 3¼".

From the burgundy binding print, cut:
8 strips, each 2½" x 42", for binding

DIRECTIONS

Patterns for the blocks are on pages 25–32 and 49–72.

Appliqué the Blocks

Follow the directions for the twenty-block quilt on page 15. Trim the squares to 14" x 14", keeping the design centered.

Assemble the Quilt Top

1. Sew the block and sashing pieces together in horizontal rows. Make 4 rows.

2. Sew the remaining sashing and cornerstone pieces together to make 5 rows.

3. Join the rows.

Attach the Borders and Add Border Appliqués

1. Add the border strips to the quilt top, mitering the corners. See "Mitered-Corner Borders" on page 21.
2. Appliqué the pieces for the border in a manner similar to the twenty-block quilt, except cut the swag from one piece of fabric and omit the rosebuds.

Mark the Quilting Patterns

Mark the feather quilting patterns on the border inside the swag pieces. Place the longer feather pattern (A) at the corners, and the shorter feather pattern (B) along the sides of the quilt as shown below.

The rest of the quilting does not need to be marked. Outline-quilt around all the appliqué shapes and around the edges of the sashing and cornerstones. Stipple-quilt in the background areas of the blocks and border.

Finish the Quilt

Layer, baste, bind, and finish the quilt in the same manner as for the twenty-block quilt.

Feather pattern A   Feather pattern B

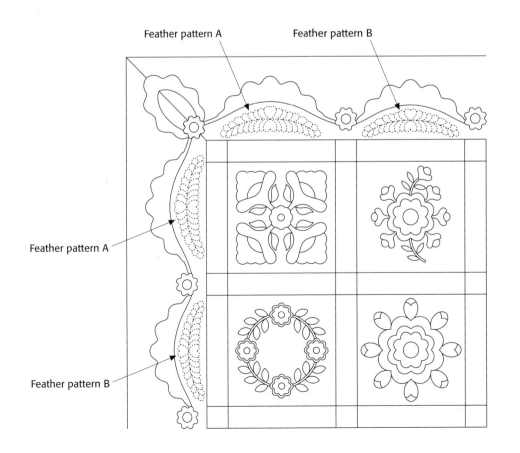

Feather pattern A

Feather pattern B

Quilt Finishing

Squaring Up Blocks

Some quiltmakers find it necessary to trim or square up their blocks before they assemble them into a quilt top. If you trim, be sure to leave ¼" seam allowances beyond any points or other important block details that fall at the outside edges of the block.

To square up blocks, cut a piece of plastic-coated freezer paper to the proper size (finished block size plus seam allowance); iron the freezer paper to your ironing-board cover, plastic side down. Pin the block edges to the edges of the freezer-paper guide and gently press with steam; allow the blocks to cool before you unpin and remove them.

Adding Borders

For best results, do not cut border strips and sew them directly to the quilt sides without measuring first. The edges of a quilt often measure slightly longer than the distance through the quilt center, due to stretching during construction. Instead, measure the quilt top through the center in both directions to determine how long to cut the border strips. This step ensures that the finished quilt will be as straight and as square as possible, without wavy edges.

Mitered-Corner Borders

1. First estimate the finished outside dimensions of your quilt, including borders. Border strips should be cut to this length plus at least ½" for seam allowances; it's safer to add 3" to 4" for some leeway.
2. Fold the quilt in half and mark the center of the quilt edges. Fold each border strip in half and mark the center with a pin.
3. Measure the length and width of the quilt top across the center. Note the measurements.

4. Place a pin at each end of the side border strips to mark the length of the quilt top. Repeat with the top and bottom border strips.

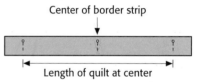

5. Pin the border strips to the quilt top, matching the centers. Line up the pins at each end of the border strip with the edges of the quilt. Stitch, beginning and ending the stitching ¼" from the raw edges of the quilt top. Repeat with the remaining border strips.

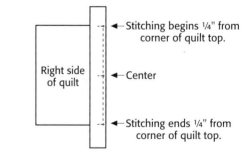

6. Lay the first corner to be mitered on the ironing board. Fold under one border strip at a 45° angle to the other strip. Press and pin.

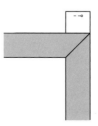

7. Fold the quilt with right sides together, lining up the edges of the border. If necessary, use a ruler to draw a pencil line on the crease to make the line more visible. Stitch on the crease, sewing from the corner to the outside edge.

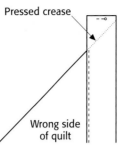
Pressed crease
Wrong side of quilt

8. Press the seam open and trim away the excess from the border strips, leaving a ¼"-wide seam allowance.
9. Repeat with the remaining corners.

Marking the Quilting Lines

Whether or not to mark the quilting designs depends upon the type of quilting you will be doing. Marking is not necessary if you plan to quilt in-the-ditch or outline-quilt a uniform distance from the seam lines. For more complex quilting designs, mark the quilt top before the quilt is layered with batting and backing.

Choose a marking tool that will be visible on your fabric and test it on fabric scraps to be sure the marks can be removed easily. Masking tape can be used to mark straight quilting. Tape only small sections at a time and remove the tape when you stop at the end of the day; otherwise, the sticky residue may be difficult to remove from the fabric

Layering the Quilt

The quilt "sandwich" consists of backing, batting, and the quilt top. Cut the quilt backing at least 4" larger than the quilt top all the way around. For large quilts, it is usually necessary to sew two or three lengths of fabric together to make a backing of the required size. Trim away the selvages before piecing the lengths together. Press seams open to make quilting easier.

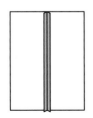
Two lengths of fabric seamed in the center

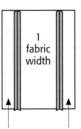
1 fabric width
Partial fabric width

Batting comes packaged in standard bed sizes, or it can be purchased by the yard. Several weights or thicknesses are available. Thick battings are fine for tied quilts and comforters; a thinner batting is better, however, if you intend to quilt by hand or machine.

To put it all together:
1. Spread the backing, wrong side up, on a flat, clean surface. Anchor it with pins or masking tape. Be careful not to stretch the backing out of shape.
2. Spread the batting over the backing, smoothing out any wrinkles.
3. Place the pressed quilt top on top of the batting, right side up. Smooth out any wrinkles and make sure the quilt-top edges are parallel to the backing edges.
4. Starting in the center, baste with needle and thread and work diagonally to each corner. Continue basting in a grid of horizontal and vertical lines 6" to 8" apart. Finish by basting around the edges.

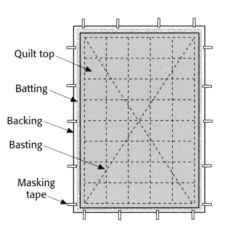
Quilt top
Batting
Backing
Basting
Masking tape

NOTE
For machine quilting, you may baste the layers with #2 rustproof safety pins. Place pins about 6" to 8" apart, away from the area you intend to quilt.

Hand Quilting

To quilt by hand, you will need short, sturdy needles (called "Betweens"), quilting thread, and a thimble to fit the middle finger of your sewing hand. Use the smallest needle you can comfortably handle; the finer the needle, the smaller your stitches will be. Most quilters also use a frame or hoop to support their work.

1. Thread your needle with a single strand of quilting thread about 18" long; make a small knot and insert the needle in the top layer about 1" from where you want to start stitching. Pull the needle out at the point where you want to begin quilting and gently pull the thread until the knot pops through the fabric and into the batting.

2. Take small, evenly spaced stitches through all three quilt layers.

3. Rock the needle up and down through all layers, until you have 3 or 4 stitches on the needle. Place your other hand underneath the quilt so you can feel the needle point with the tip of your finger when a stitch is taken.

4. To end a line of quilting, make a small knot close to the last stitch; backstitch, running the thread a needle's length through the batting. Gently pull the thread until the knot pops into the batting; clip the thread at the quilt's surface.

For more information on hand quilting, refer to *Loving Stitches* by Jeana Kimball (That Patchwork Place).

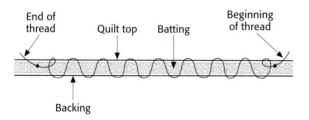

End of thread   Quilt top   Batting   Beginning of thread

Backing

Machine Quilting

Machine quilting is suitable for all types of quilts, from crib to full-size bed quilts. With machine quilting, you can quickly complete quilts that might otherwise languish on the shelves.

Marking is only necessary if you need to follow a grid or a complex pattern. It is not necessary if you plan to quilt in-the-ditch, outline-quilt a uniform distance from seam lines, or free-motion-quilt in a random pattern over the quilt surface or in selected areas.

1. For straight-line quilting, it is extremely helpful to have a walking foot to help feed the quilt layers through the machine without shifting or puckering. Some machines have a built-in walking foot; other machines require a separate attachment.

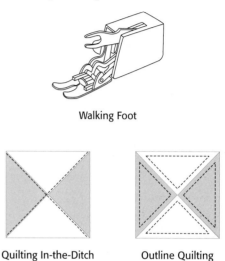

Walking Foot

Quilting In-the-Ditch   Outline Quilting

2. For free-motion quilting, you need a darning foot and the ability to drop the feed dogs on your machine. With free-motion quilting, you do not turn the fabric under the needle but instead guide the fabric in the direction of the design. Use free-motion quilting to outline-quilt a fabric motif or to create stippling or other curved designs.

Darning Foot

Free-Motion Quilting

Binding

For a French double-fold binding, cut 2½"-wide strips from the straight grain of the fabric. You will need enough strips to go around the perimeter of the quilt plus 10" for seams and mitered corners.

To attach binding:

1. Sew strips, right sides together, to make one long piece of binding. Press seams open. Join strips at right angles and stitch across the corner as shown. Trim excess fabric and press seams open.

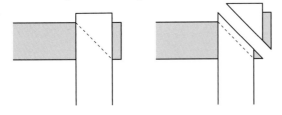

Joining Straight-cut Strips

2. Trim one end of the strip at a 45° angle. Turn under ¼" and press.
3. Fold the strip in half lengthwise, wrong sides together, and press.

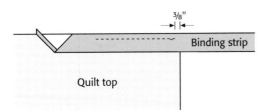

Fold line

4. Trim batting and backing even with the quilt top.
5. Starting on one side of the quilt and using a ⅜"-wide seam allowance, stitch the binding to the quilt, keeping the raw edges even with the quilt-top edge. End the stitching ⅜" from the corner of the quilt and backstitch. Clip the thread.

⅜"

Binding strip

Quilt top

6. Turn the quilt so you will be stitching down the next side. Fold the binding up, away from the quilt, with raw edges aligned.

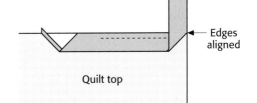

Edges aligned

Quilt top

7. Fold the binding back down onto itself, even with the edge of the quilt top. Begin stitching ⅜" from the edge, backstitching to secure.

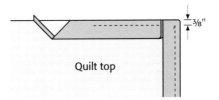

⅜"

Quilt top

8. Repeat on the remaining edges and corners of the quilt. When you reach the beginning of the binding, overlap the beginning stitches by about 1" and cut away any excess binding, trimming the end at a 45° angle. Tuck the end of the binding into the fold and finish the seam.

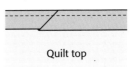

Quilt top

9. Fold the binding over the raw edges of the quilt to the back, with the folded edge covering the row of machine stitching, and blindstitch in place. A miter will form at each corner. Blindstitch the mitered corners in place.

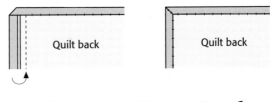

Quilt back

Quilt back

Signing Your Quilt

Be sure to sign and date your quilt. Future generations will be interested to know more than just who made it and when. Labels can be as elaborate or as simple as you desire. The information can be handwritten, typed, or embroidered. Be sure to include the name of the quilt, your name, your city and state, the date, the name of the recipient if it is a gift, and any other interesting or important information about the quilt.

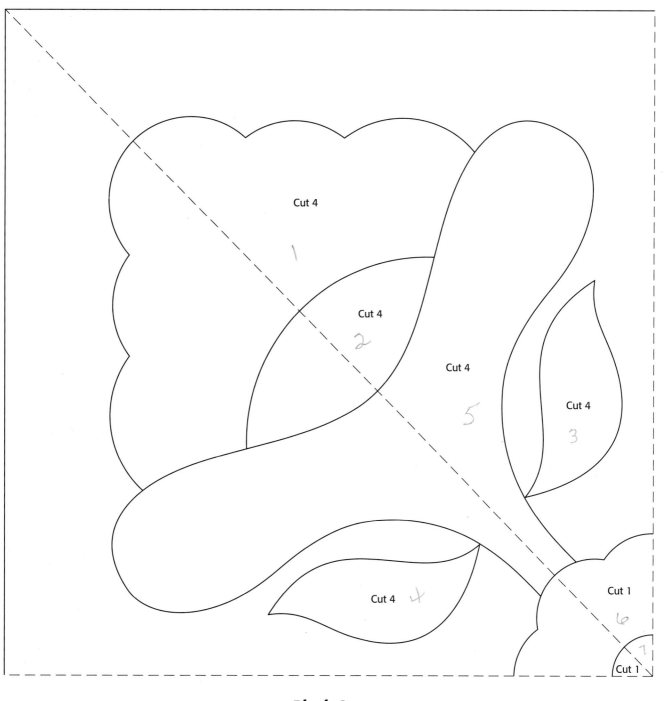

Cut 4

Cut 4

Cut 4

Cut 4

Cut 4

Cut 1

Cut 1

Block One
Indiana Rose
Variation

Fabric Tip: For added interest, use two different green prints, one for the main flower stalk and another for the smaller leaves.

Position appliqués, working from the outside of the block toward the center so that each new piece overlaps the raw edge of the preceding one. This order works for most appliqué flower patterns, such as this one.

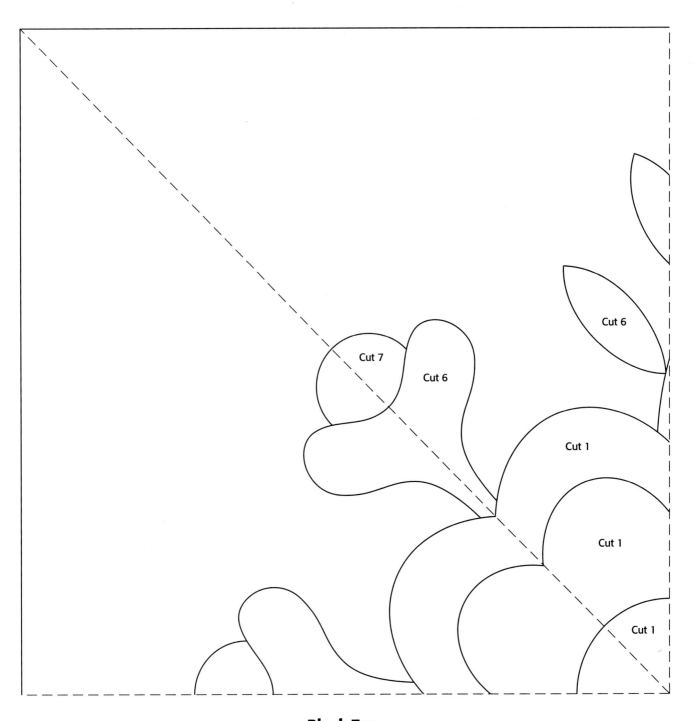

Block Two
Rose of Sharon
Variation #1
Upper left quadrant

Fabric Tip: For variety, use two different green prints, one for the buds and stem and another for the leaves.

As a general rule, if you are using the freezer-paper appliqué method for the stems, always trace their shapes from the reverse side of the pattern to ensure that they will curve in the correct direction. This is true of all asymmetrical shapes.

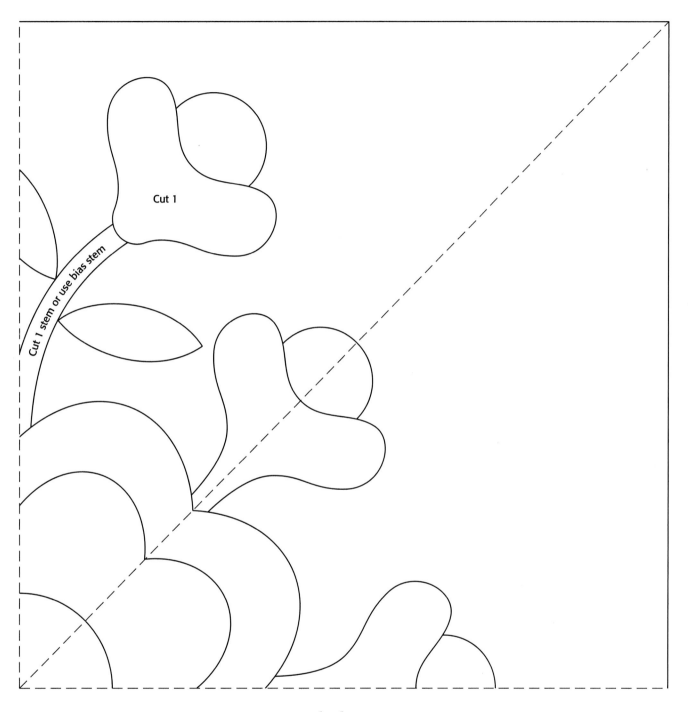

Cut 1

Cut 1 stem or use bias stem

Block Two
Rose of Sharon
Variation #1
Upper right quadrant

Block Two
Rose of Sharon
Variation #1
Lower left quadrant

Cut 1 stem or use bias stem

Block Two
Rose of Sharon
Variation #1
Lower right quadrant

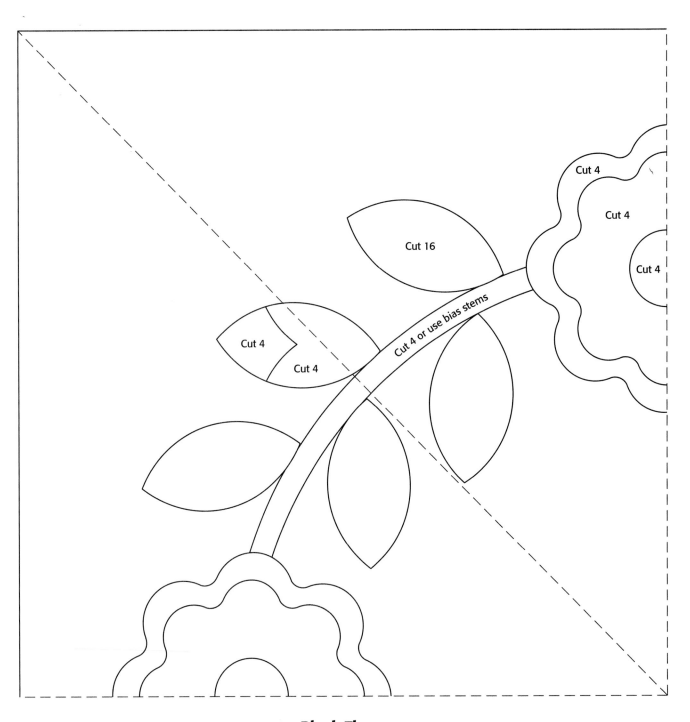

Cut 4

Cut 4

Cut 4

Cut 16

Cut 4 or use bias stems

Cut 4

Cut 4

Block Three
Wreath of Roses
Upper left and lower right quadrants

Appliqué the stems first and cover the ends with the flowers. To remove
freezer paper from the stem, make a continuous slit in the block behind the stem.
Remove the freezer paper. It is not necessary to trim any of the background block
behind the stems.

Block Three
Wreath of Roses
Upper right and lower left quadrants

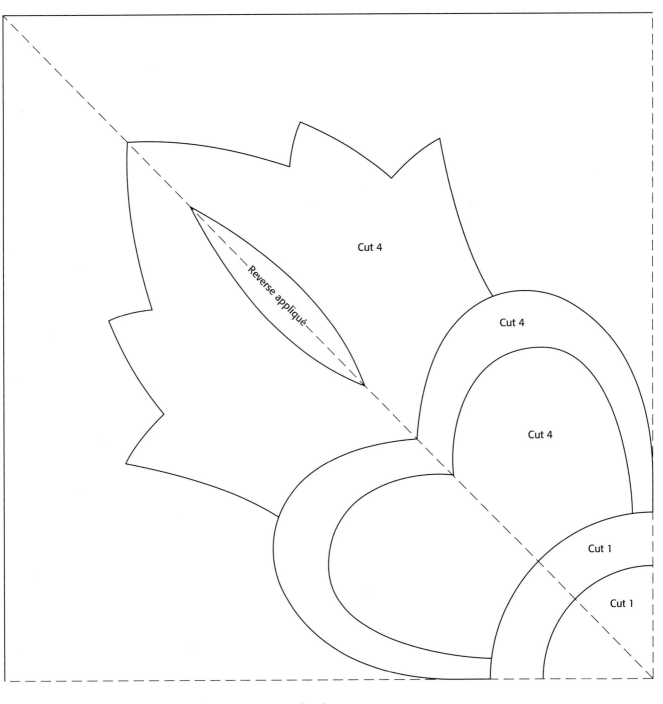

Cut 4

Reverse appliqué

Cut 4

Cut 4

Cut 1

Cut 1

Block Four
Lancaster Rose

Use reverse appliqué for the spaces in the center
of the leaves so the background fabric shows through.

Quilt Gallery

Rose Sampler Supreme by Rosemary Makhan, 1992, 84" x 100", Burlington, Ontario.

Block One
Indiana Rose Variation

Block Two
Rose of Sharon Variation #1

Block Three
Wreath of Roses

Block Four
Lancaster Rose

Block Five
Rose and Tulip Variation

Block Six
Rose of Sharon Variation #2

Block Seven
Ohio Rose

Block Eight
Ring Around the Roses

Block Nine
Rosebud Wreath

Block Ten
Rose of Sharon Variation #3

Block Eleven
Prairie Rose

Block Twelve
Wild Rose Wreath

Block Thirteen
Democrat Rose

Block Fourteen
Spring Wreath

Block Fifteen
Rose of Sharon Variation #4

Block Sixteen
American Beauty Rose

Block Seventeen
Tudor Rose

Block Eighteen
President's Wreath

Block Nineteen
Wild Rose

Block Twenty
Whig Rose

Rose Sampler Supreme,
border and corner detail

Roses for Travis and Sharon by Peggy Gelbrich, 1996, 83" x 98", Ketchikan, Alaska.
This quilt was a wedding gift for Peggy's son, Travis, and his wife, Sharon Rose.
It won the Best of Show award at the Quilting In The Rain V show in 1996.

Rose Sampler Twelve-Block Variation by Rosemary Makhan,
pieced in 1991 and quilted in 1999, 72" x 88", Burlington, Ontario.

Rose of Sharon by Barbara Green, 1999, 92" x 103", Brampton, Ontario.
This quilt won Grand Champion at the Brampton Fall Fair 1999 and
President's Choice at the Brampton Quilter's Guild Show.

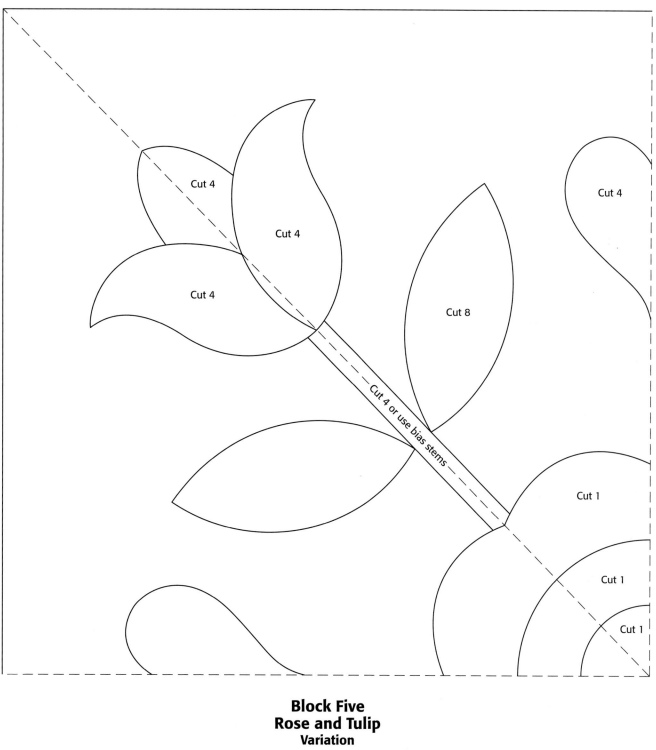

**Block Five
Rose and Tulip
Variation**

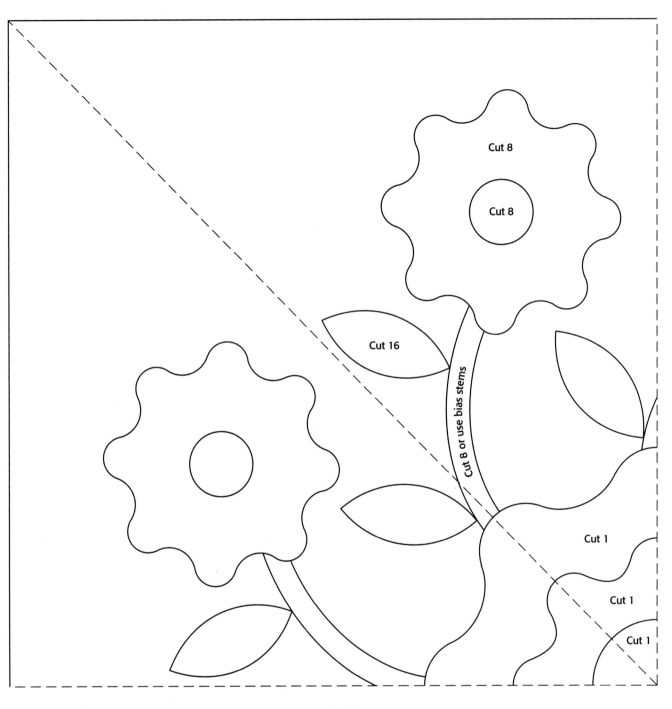

Cut 8

Cut 8

Cut 16

Cut 8 or use bias stems

Cut 1

Cut 1

Cut 1

Block Six
Rose of Sharon
Variation #2

Be sure to reverse pattern to trace the curved stems
if using the freezer-paper appliqué method.

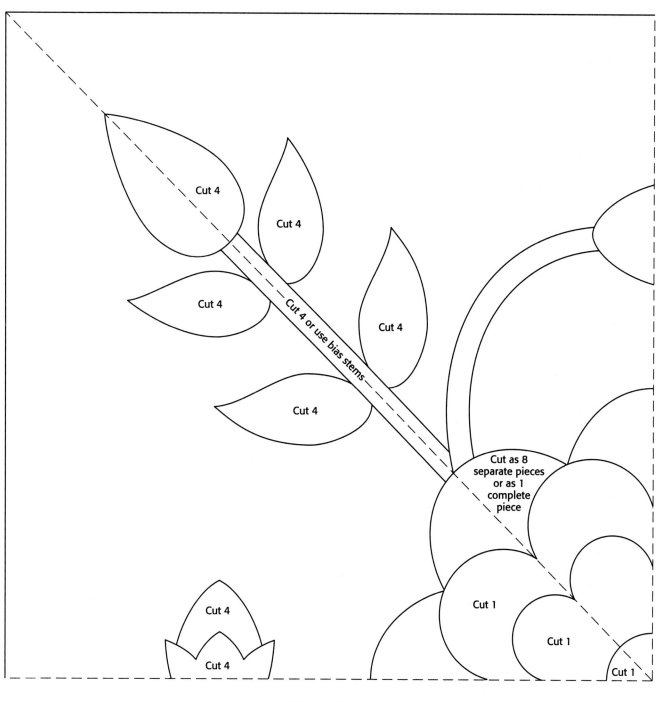

Cut 4

Cut 4

Cut 4

Cut 4

Cut 4 or use bias stems

Cut 4

Cut 4

Cut as 8 separate pieces or as 1 complete piece

Cut 4

Cut 4

Cut 1

Cut 1

Cut 1

Block Seven
Ohio Rose

Be sure to reverse pattern to trace the curved stems
if using the freezer-paper appliqué method.

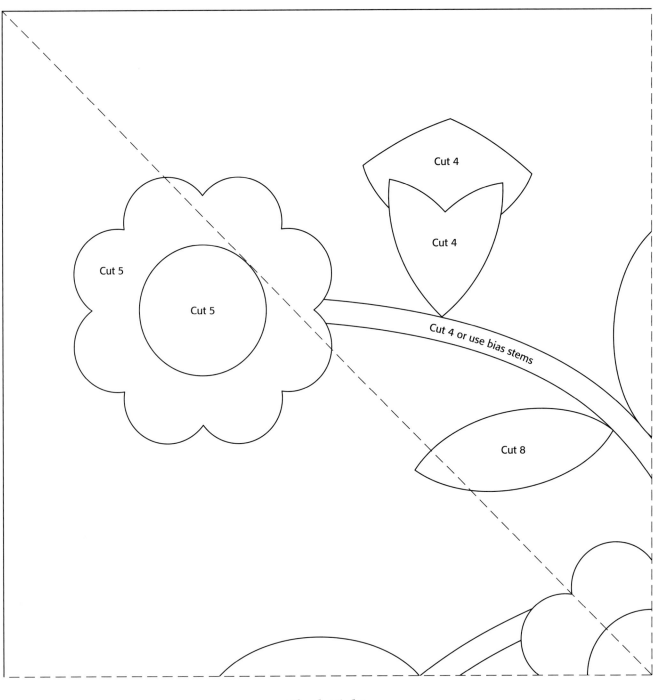

Cut 4

Cut 4

Cut 5

Cut 5

Cut 4 or use bias stems

Cut 8

**Block Eight
Ring Around the Roses**

Cut 1—all in one piece

Cut 5

Cut 26

Cut 8

Cut 13

Block Nine
Rosebud Wreath
Upper left quadrant

Fabric Tip: The wreath will look more colorful if each entire bud is made in shades of the flower color.

Trace the buds from the reverse side of the pattern to ensure that the angle at the base will be correct.

It is best to use the freezer-paper method to appliqué the wreath stem. That way, it will be cut in a continuous piece, and a joining seam will not be necessary as it would be with a bias strip.

Block Nine
Rosebud Wreath
Upper right quadrant

Block Nine
Rosebud Wreath
Lower left quadrant

Block Nine
Rosebud Wreath
Lower right quadrant

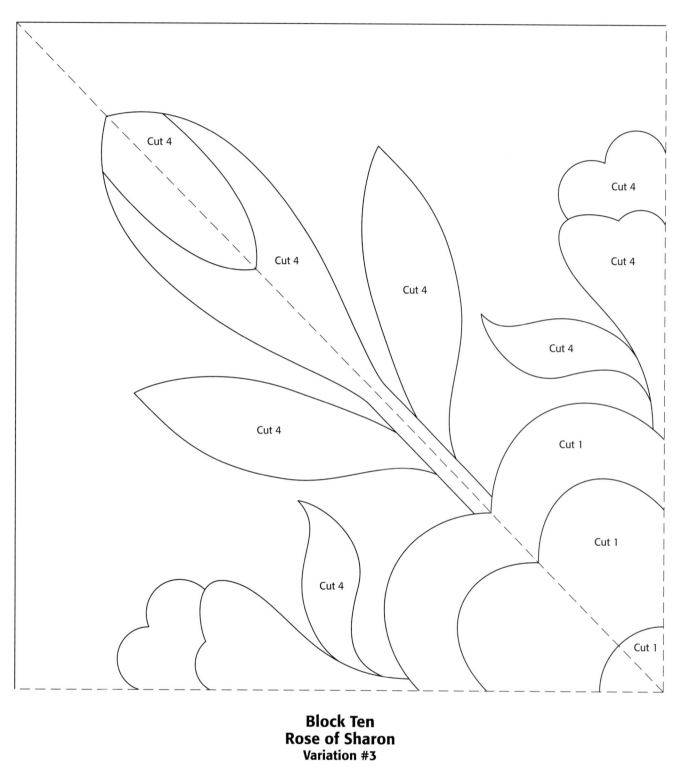

Cut 4

Cut 4

Cut 4

Cut 4

Cut 4

Cut 4

Cut 4

Cut 1

Cut 4

Cut 1

Cut 1

Block Ten
Rose of Sharon
Variation #3

If desired, the alternate bud shape can be used. It is easier to appliqué than the shape shown above because it does not have the long, sharp points.

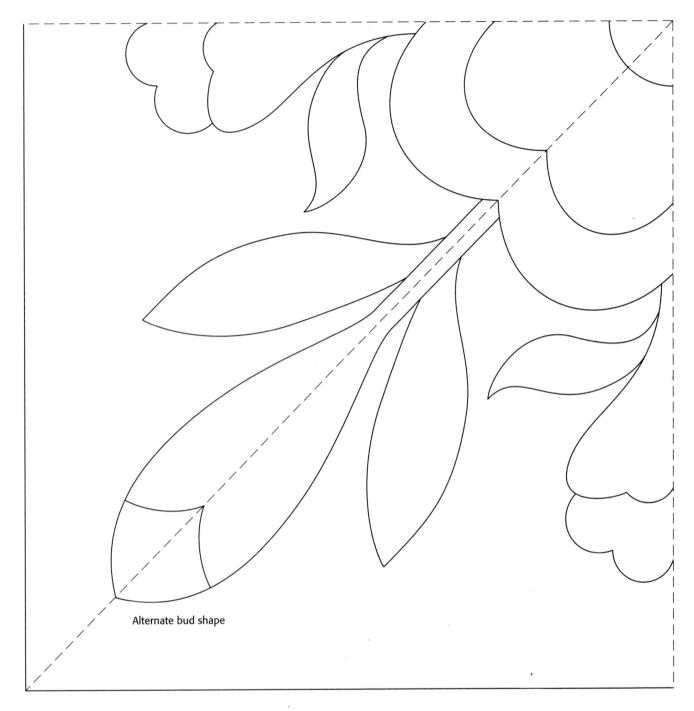

Alternate bud shape

Block Ten
Rose of Sharon
Variation #3
Alternate bud shape

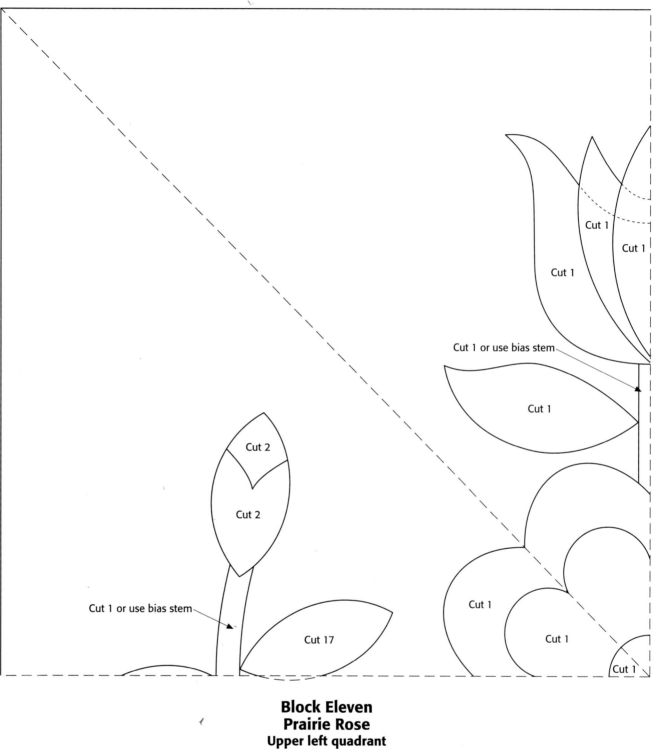

Cut 1

Cut 1

Cut 1

Cut 1

Cut 1 or use bias stem

Cut 1

Cut 2

Cut 2

Cut 1 or use bias stem

Cut 17

Cut 1

Cut 1

Cut 1

Block Eleven
Prairie Rose
Upper left quadrant

Cut 1

Block Eleven
Prairie Rose
Upper right quadrant

Block Eleven
Prairie Rose
Lower left quadrant

Block Eleven
Prairie Rose
Lower right quadrant

Cut 20

Cut 16

Cut 16

Cut 4

Cut 4 or use bias stems

**Block Twelve
Wild Rose Wreath**

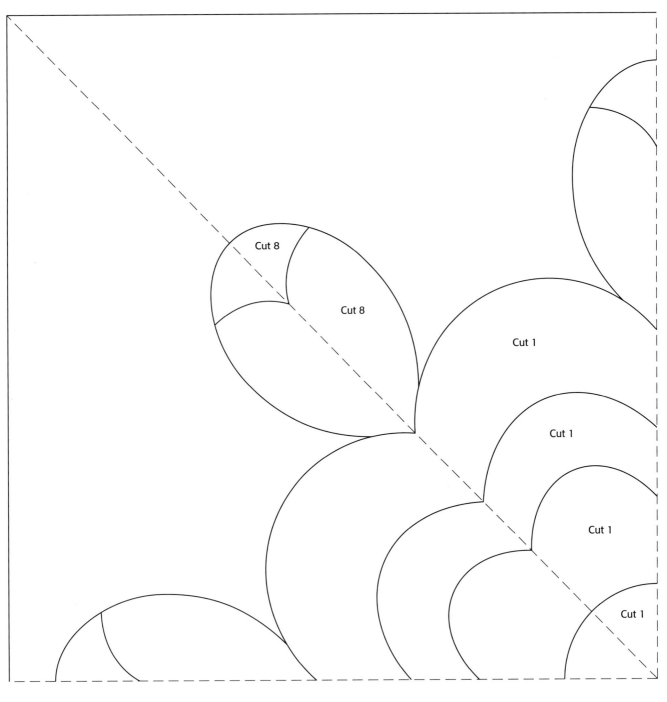

Cut 8

Cut 8

Cut 1

Cut 1

Cut 1

Cut 1

**Block Thirteen
Democrat Rose**

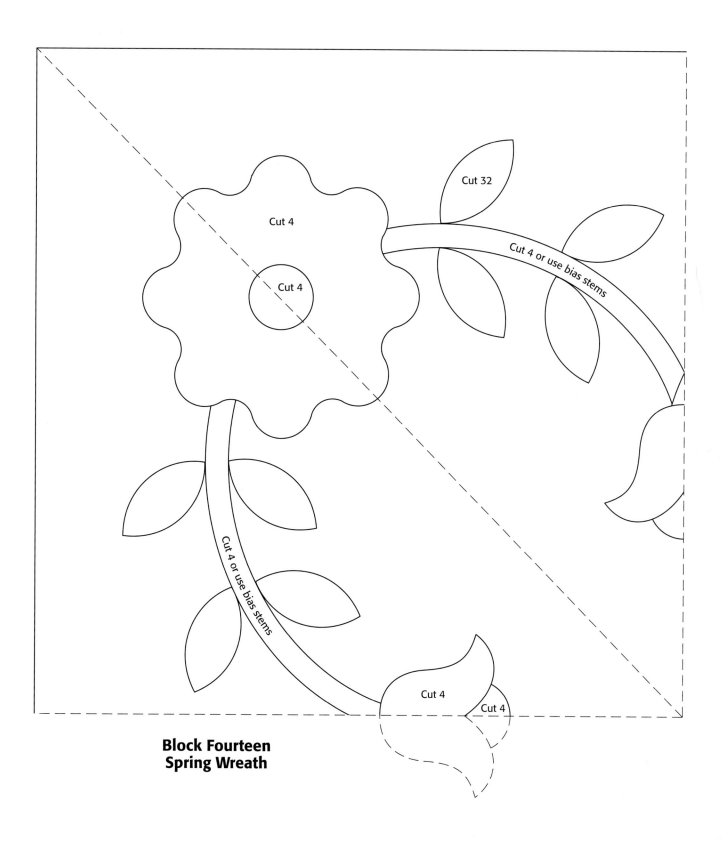

Cut 32

Cut 4

Cut 4

Cut 4 or use bias stems

Cut 4 or use bias stems

Cut 4

Cut 4

Block Fourteen
Spring Wreath

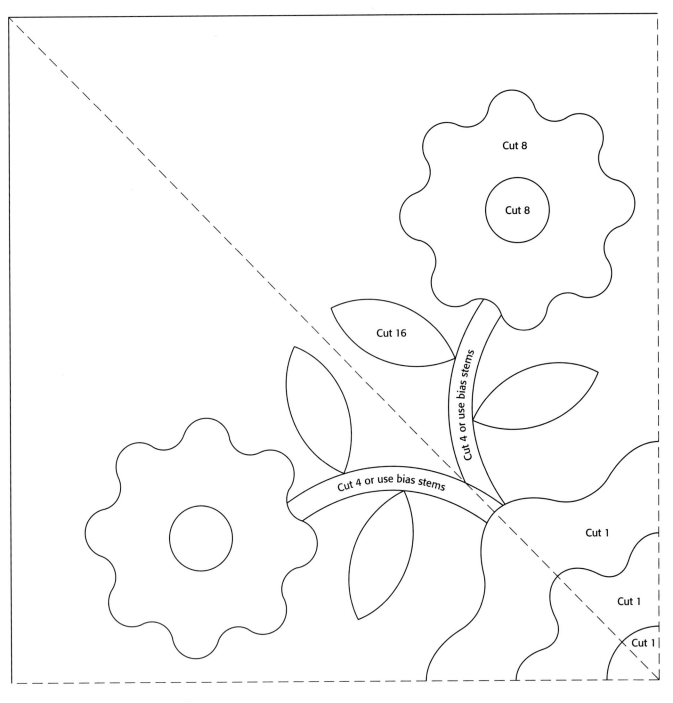

Cut 8

Cut 8

Cut 16

Cut 4 or use bias stems

Cut 4 or use bias stems

Cut 1

Cut 1

Cut 1

Block Fifteen
Rose of Sharon
Variation #4

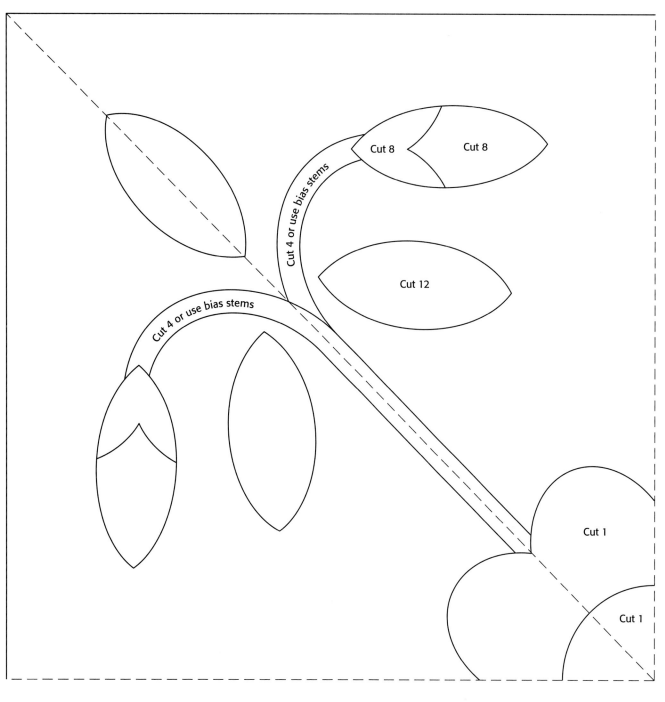

Cut 8

Cut 8

Cut 4 or use bias stems

Cut 12

Cut 4 or use bias stems

Cut 1

Cut 1

**Block Sixteen
American Beauty Rose**

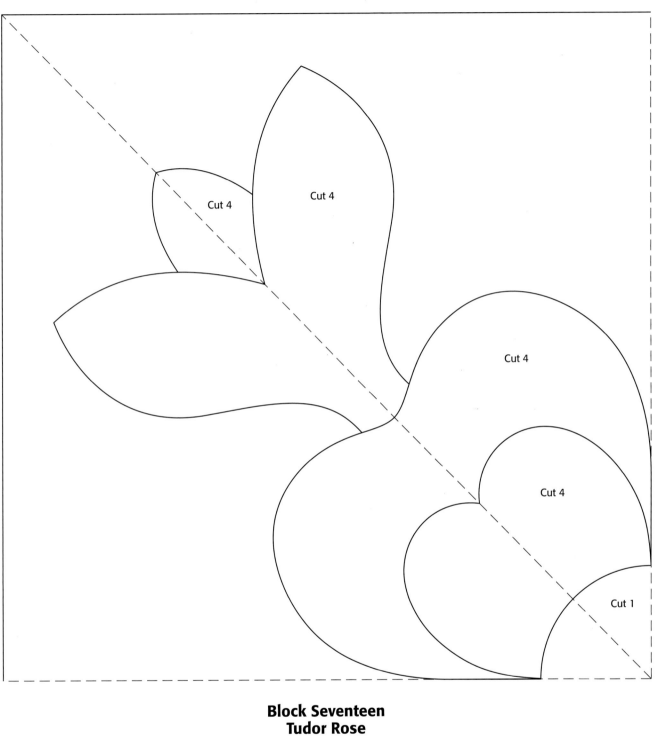

Cut 4

Cut 4

Cut 4

Cut 4

Cut 1

Block Seventeen
Tudor Rose

Cut 12

Cut 4

Cut 4

Cut 16

Cut 4 or use bias stems

Cut 4

Cut 4

Cut 4

Cut 4

Block Eighteen
President's Wreath

If using the freezer-paper method, trace the buds from the reverse side
of the pattern to get the correct angle on the stems.

Cut 2

Cut 2

Cut 8

Cut 8

Cut 2

Block Nineteen
Wild Rose
Upper left and lower right quadrants

Use reverse appliqué for the slits to allow the background fabric to show through the leaves.

Reverse the pattern to draw the buds and leaves if using the freezer-paper method.

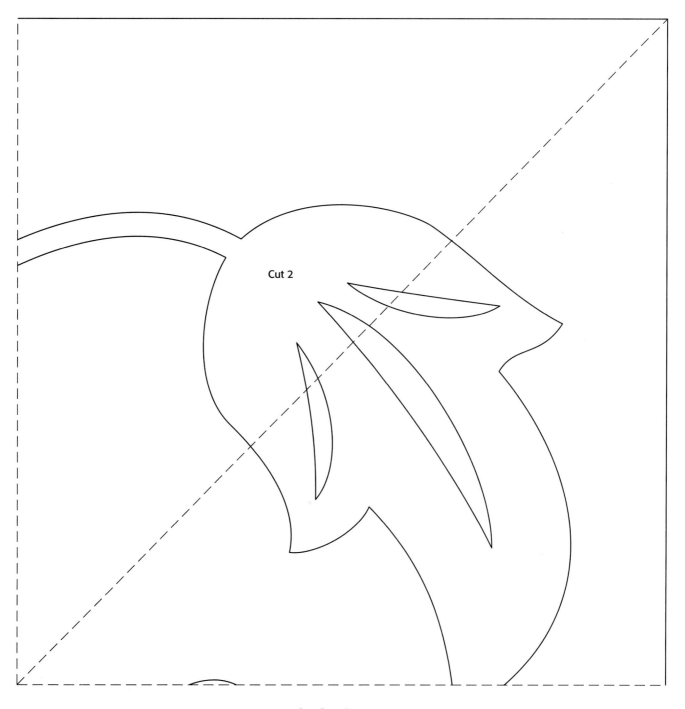

Cut 2

Block Nineteen
Wild Rose
Upper right and lower left quadrants

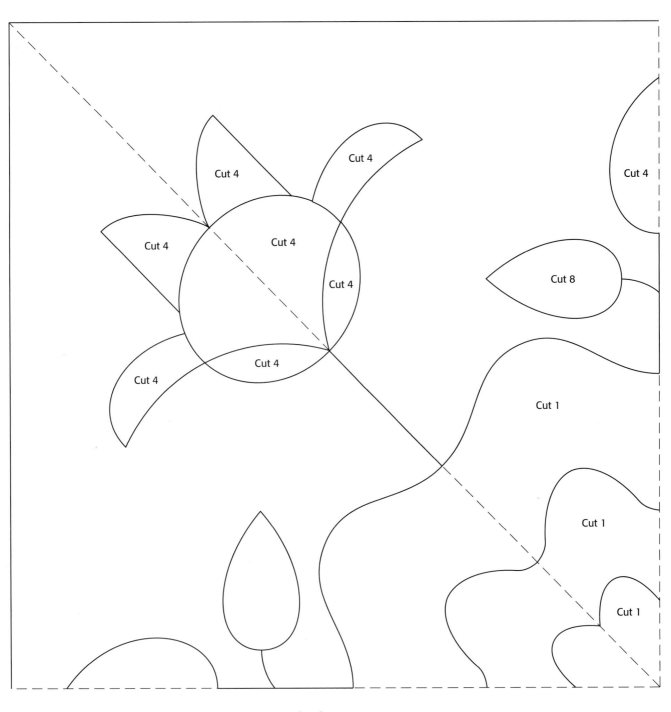

Cut 4

Cut 4

Cut 4

Cut 4

Cut 4

Cut 8

Cut 4

Cut 4

Cut 1

Cut 1

Cut 1

Block Twenty
Whig Rose

Embroider the solid lines (stems) that connect the flowers and leaf clusters to the central rose. Use the stem stitch shown on page 00, using 3 strands of embroidery floss. You can also make very narrow bias stems if you prefer.

Border Appliqué Shapes

Use the longer swag pieces at each corner of the quilt where extra length is needed. Trim swag pieces as necessary.

If you wish and you have ample yardage, you may cut the swags all in one piece from one fabric instead of two different fabrics as shown.

Place the flowers in line with the ends of the sashing pieces and at the four corners where the swags meet.

Center the buds inside the swags along each border. Refer to the quilt photo for placement, noting that all the buds flow in the same direction around the quilt.

When appliquéing the swag, let the outer swag piece tuck up under the inner swag piece.

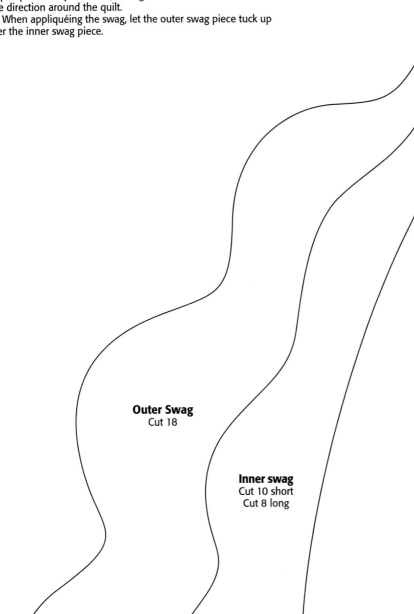

Cut here for the
shorter swag pieces.

Outer Swag
Cut 18

Inner swag
Cut 10 short
Cut 8 long

Center line

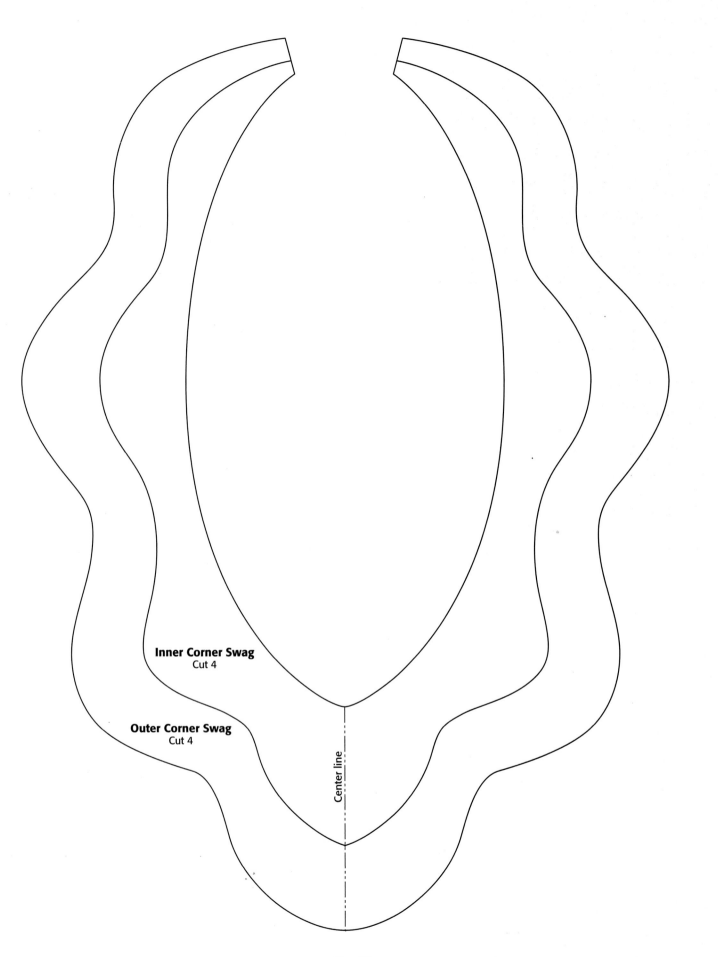

Inner Corner Swag
Cut 4

Outer Corner Swag
Cut 4

Center line

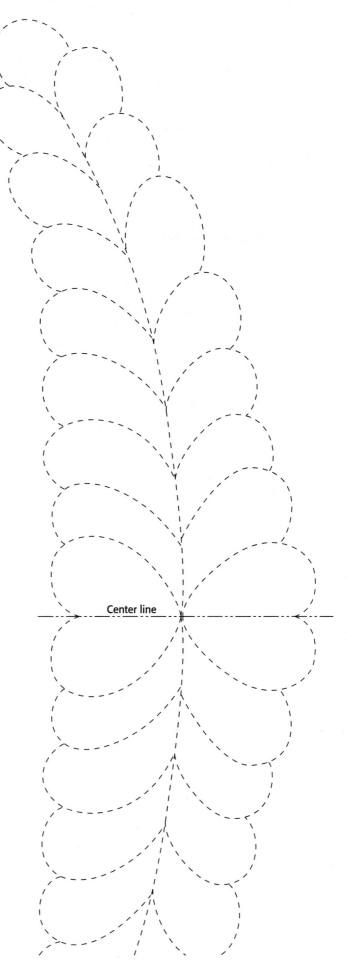

Quilting Pattern B
for 12-Block Variation

Position ¼" from sashing
between sashing and appliquéd swags
along sides of quilt.

Center line

About the Author

Rosemary Makhan grew up in Nova Scotia, where she learned the basics of quiltmaking from her mother. Her love of sewing and fabric led her to major in home economics at Acadia University, and she taught high school Family Studies for several years.

Her interest in quiltmaking was rekindled when she made a baby quilt for her daughter, Candice. She began teaching adult-education quilting classes and was the founder of the local Halton Quilters' Guild. Rosemary now teaches many classes and workshops and enjoys the special fellowship and inspiration that comes from working with quilters.

A traditional quiltmaker, Rosemary loves appliqué but makes many pieced quilts as well. Often the quilts are of her own design, but if not, she changes or adds something to make them distinctive.

Rosemary lives in Burlington, Ontario, Canada, with her husband, Chris. They have two children, Candice and Kenneth.